WRECKS & RE

RANGE TARGETS

Silhouetted against the rolling hills this range target was
on the Sennybridge Ranges in Wales. A battered Daimler
armoured car stands guard to the open, upland moor.

MARK KHAN

To find out about other titles produced by
Historic Military Press visit our website at www.historicmilitarypress.com.
Alternatively please write to us free of charge at
Customer Services, Historic Military Press,
Freepost SEA 11014, Pulborough, West Sussex, RH20 4BR,
or telephone our freephone number: 0800 071 7419.

HISTORIC MILITARY PRESS

RANGE TARGETS

© Copyright Mark Khan, 2001.

First published 2001 by Historic Military Press,

ISBN 1-901313-09-3

I wish to thank the following people, in no particular order, without whom this book would not have been possible. The staff of Headquarters Army Training Estate (Salisbury Plain); Headquarters Army Training Estate (Wales); and the Defence Estates Organisation (Brecon and Salisbury Plain). Jonathan Jackson for countless hours of assistance and good companionship. Bob Stephens for the Daimler photographs and Tim Chance for the 'Stug' and Jagdpanther pictures. Martin Mace for providing impetus and encouragement to write this book.

Writing a book of this nature has required much in-depth research into the various types and designs which are covered. To this end mention must be made to the following authors (and their books) for having had the foresight to write these excellent reference guides. 'Tanks and other Armoured Fighting Vehicles of World War II', B.T. White, Peerage Books, London, 1983. 'The illustrated encyclopedia of Artillery', Ian V. Hogg, Guild Publishing, London, 1987. 'World War II Tanks', Eric Grove, Black Cat, London, 1987. 'The Great Tanks', C. Ellis & P. Chamberlain, Hamlyn, London, 1975. 'World War Two Military Vehicles - Transport & Halftracks', G.N. Georgano, Osprey Automotive, London, 1994. Armoured Fighting Vehicles of the World, Christopher F. Foss, Ian Allan, Shepperton, 1977. 'Churchill's Secret Weapons', Patrick Delaforce, Robert Hale, London, 1998. 'British Military Vehicles', The Fighting Vehicles Research and Development Establishment, Chertsey, 1966. 'Tanks and fighting vehicles', C.F. Foss, Salamander, London, 1977. 'Small arms, artillery and special weapons of the Third Reich', T. Gander and P. Chamberlain, Macdonald & James, London. 'British and American Tanks of World War 2', P. Chamberlain and C. Ellis, Arms & Armour Press, London. 'British Military aircraft serials 1911-1979', Bruce Robertson, Patrick Stephens Ltd., London. 'The Guns, 1939-1945', Ian V. Hogg, Purnell, London. 'A history of the Gunnery Wing - Royal School of Artillery', Lt.-Col. (TIG) J.R. Guy RA, unpublished.

Mark Khan is an accomplished military historian, and has previously written for magazines and journals such as 'After the Battle'. It was his position as the Official Historian for the Sennybridge Ranges in Wales that provided the inspiration behind this book. His particular interest in military history, alongside British military ranges, includes ammunition and its packaging and Second World War field rations.

Printed in the United Kingdom by
Selsey Press Ltd., 84 High Street, Selsey, Chichester, PO20 0QH
Telephone: 01243 605234

HISTORIC MILITARY PRESS
Green Arbor, Rectory Road, Storrington, West Sussex, RH20 4EF. Telephone/Fax: 01903 741941

www.historicmilitarypress.com

RANGE TARGETS

When military vehicles are no longer required, a variety of fates might befall them. They may be sold into civilian ownership, passed onto the military forces of another nation, scrapped or put into store. Some however, may continue to "serve", becoming targets or training features on military training areas. Some are also left forgotten on ex-military training areas, rusting away hidden in the woods. Many of the military training areas that are still in use, by their nature (due to lack of public access), often become "time-capsules", where the landscape and environment may have changed little since the time it came into military use. Often this can be graphically illustrated from the air, by the change in landscape where the boundary between privately owned land and Military land can be easily seen. Much military land has remained free from the effects of intensive farming and housing development and consequently has preserved many ecological, archaeological, and landscape features. Amongst these preserved features can be found examples of military vehicles.

Even on military training areas that are no longer in use and that have reverted back to private or public ownership, some old range targets and features may still remain. Often due to the sheer bulk of these targets, the difficulty of removing them has often led to them remaining intact or buried insitu. This is particularly true of training areas used during the Second World War. Even when these targets have been removed, with careful observation evidence may still be found in the form of smaller remains (e.g. tank bogie wheels, pieces of tank track). For example, on one particular ex-Home Guard training area the remains of a Valentine tank still remain scattered around a chalk pit (probably due to the effect of countless hours of demolition training). It may seem peculiar to find these relics scattered around the British countryside, but one has to take into account the mindset at the end of the war and for some time after. Then, these vehicles would have been commonplace, (familiarity breeds contempt), and there existed, (understandably), a common desire to forget the war. These training areas would have held no interest to the public at large other than perhaps the curiosity of the younger generations!

Military vehicles, are generally split into 2 categories:
        "A" Vehicles - Armoured or lightly armoured vehicles (e.g. tanks, armoured personnel carriers)
        "B" Vehicles - Non-armoured vehicles (e.g. lorries, light vehicles)
These vehicles, once they become targets/training features, are subject to the ravages of weather, time and of course the results of direct fire. The armoured targets, as one would expect, often fare better than the soft targets, but is surprising how many of each type still remain. On military training areas one will find vehicles that have been in service long ago, to those more recently in current service. These vehicles represent a silent tribute to the men that fought in them, from places as diverse as the Libyan Desert to the streets of Northern Ireland. They serve as reminders of times when grit, determination, self-sacrifice and courage were the order of the day. As we flick through the pages of this book, we would do well to remember those who made the ultimate sacrifice in the service of their country.

This book is a brief, though by no means complete, trip through what is or until recently was, lurking in the British countryside. It is vital to remember that where vehicles reside on Ministry of Defence land they are strictly out of bounds to the general public. Military training areas are dangerous places (not only in terms of the live firing, but also tactical vehicle movements) and one must never attempt to enter without permission. To the military archeologist, historian or military vehicle enthusiastic the following pictures will no doubt fire the curiosity in relation to the history of the vehicles. Unfortunately, often little is known about the history of the vehicles in this book. Where details are known, they have been included. To comprehensively research the background of each vehicle would be a major task, so no attempt has been made to do so. It will be left to the reader to contemplate what the history of each of these vehicles may be - if they could talk, no doubt some very interesting stories they would tell!

1

GERMAN ARTILLERY

The Russian Steppe? - No Wiltshire !!!, These WW2 German guns have been used as targets on Salisbury Plain. There are 6 altogether: 3 x 150mm (15 cm schwere Feldhaubitze 18) and 3 x 105mm (schwere 10 cm Kanone 18), laid out in a simulated battery position. Positive proof can be established on one of the guns, where on the breech the 3-character manufacturer's code can be seen. This reads 'cyq'- Metalwaren Fabrik - Spreewerk Berlin Spandau. Little is known about these guns. Whilst trying to establish the identity on one of these guns, by scraping away some lichen on the breech, I came across remnants of sand coloured paint. One of the other guns has traces of field grey paint. It may be these guns were captured examples, used for evaluation. Once the Trials were complete, they were probably located on the range as targets. On the 13th May 1943, the German Afrika-Korps in North Africa surrendered. Huge numbers of men, estimated at about 175,000, were taken prisoner, along with enormous quantities of equipment. This included some 130 tanks, 300+ aircraft and in the region of 400 artillery pieces. It may well be that the sand-coloured paint indicates that one of the guns was captured in North Africa as a part of this vast haul. The example in **picture 1** is one of the 10cm Kanone 18s, normally referred to as the K18. First developed

2

in 1938, this gun could fire a shell weighing just over 15kg some 19km. With a rate of fire of 6 rounds per minute, it weighed 5642kg when in action. It is interesting to note that this example is in the fully recoiled position. The next of the artillery pieces illustrated, **2**, is the 15cm schwere Feldhaubitze 18, again more normally known as the sFH18. The sFH18 was the standard divisional medium howitzer of the German armed forces during the Second World War. Like the K18, its development also began in 1934. It was capable of firing a much heavier shell, at 43.5kg, over the smaller range of 13km. No doubt as the result of the much heavier shell, the sFH18 could only manage a rate of fire of 4 rounds per minute. Comparison of the two pictures also shows another difference - the k18 has the longer barrel, being almost twice the length of the sFH18. This sFH18 is been, and his right hand is resting on the traversing wheel which in times of battle would move the gun around its 64 degree traverse from left to right. In artillery parlance, the person occupying this position on the gun is known as the gun-layer.

THE M-40

This example of a US M40 self-propelled gun, **4**, resides in Wales. This vehicle is very sturdily constructed and even though it has suffered from several direct hits, (including aircraft cannon), it is still in remarkably good condition. This type of gun served with both US and British forces (with the Royal Artillery from 1945 until 1955). Only a small number were ever in service with the British Army where it was designated 155mm SP M40. This example still has its radial engine, a Continental R-975. This type of gun had a range of upto 19000 metres and when in service, required a crew of 8 to operate it. Positioned on a high feature within the impact area on the Sennybridge ranges it is a well-known feature to those who use the ranges. These guns were known to be involved in the bombardment of Cologne during the closing stages of the war. The rear view **5** provides a good illustration of the

configured for towing and has its limber attached - this being the set of wheels to the rear. Both of the two types of artillery pieces described used the same carriage and limber on which to be fitted. **Picture 3** is of another sFH18, this time showing the rear breech assembly. This gun has been left configured for action - note the trails split apart ready to support the gun when fired. The gentleman on the left is looking through where the gun sight would have

5

tank) rounds. These rounds have a charge of high explosive with a concave shaped copper liner. On striking the target a base fuse detonates the explosive charge, the copper liner is deformed and converted into a jet of molten metal, flame and hot gas which can punch a hole through a considerable thickness of armour. The Churchill in **picture 8**, another Mark II, can also be seen not far from the South Downs Way in West Sussex. Its story is an interesting one, and which would take a whole book to be told in full. It was found buried in 1988 and recovered on a wintry day in November 1993. Its location had been known only to a few local farmers who by then were becoming increasingly fed up with

working compartment of the gun. Inside this lightly armoured superstructure some of the crew were required to operate the imposing 155mm gun.

THE CHURCHILL

Examples of Churchill tanks can be found on ranges throughout the country, at places such as Salisbury Plain, Sennybridge and the South Downs in Sussex. **Picture 6** shows an early Mk2 variant produced in 1941. This model featured a mixed turret armament of a 2pdr gun and 7.92mm Besa machine gun. On this example the vehicle serial number can still be seen on the back (T81832). **Picture 7** is a close-up of another range tank turret and shows the effects of numerous Hollow Charge HEAT (High Explosive anti

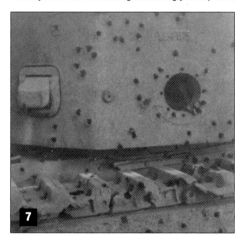

7

6

6

8

the damage the tank caused to their ploughs on a yearly basis! The members of 118 Recovery Company R.E.M.E and their skillful manipulation of two Foden wreckers achieved the recovery. This was a Territorial Army Unit, whose members had readily volunteered to undertake the challenge as a training exercise. In **picture 9** troops from 118 Recovery Company admire the upper surfaces of the Churchill as it basks in sunshine once again - the first time for nearly fifty years. At this stage in the recovery the hull has been turned over, leaving the turret, tracks and

various hatch covers in the bottom of the crater. To get this far had been no mean feat. The Warrant Officer in charge had decided that the first method of attack was to be one of the Fodens pulling on its own. Placed about 30m from the tank, its cable was pulled out and attached to the tank by a block and pulley. As the pulling strength of some 70 tons was put into action all eyes turned to the tank. However, after fifty years in one place, the Churchill seemed reluctant to move. Instead, the winch on the Foden was pulling the truck towards the tank. As the

9

10

down on the turret. It was this that provided final confirmation that it was indeed a Mark II Churchill. In its prime the turret would have carried the major armament for the tank - a 2-pounder gun with a coaxial 7.92mm Besa machine gun beside it. Another of the latter would also have been housed in the hull front. Further markings were also found on the turret. On the left hand side was a blue triangle with a clear centre. This indicated that the tank had been from 'A' Squadron. A similar triangle was also to be seen on the front right of the turret. This time the number '2' was painted in the middle in white. From this the enthusiast could interpret even more - that the tank was from the second troop, 'A' Squadron! On the hull front was a more important emblem. A block had been painted on, consisting of a blue bar above a similar sized red one. In the middle was the number '175' in white. This indicated that the tank had once been part of the Calgary Regiment, the 14th Canadian Army Tank Battalion. The Calgary Regiment was structured along the same lines as an equivalent British armoured unit. There would have been three Squadrons, each consisting three troops and, in turn, each troop would have four Churchills. When the site of this Churchill was rediscovered in 1988 almost nothing could be seen. How the tank came to be in such a position was answered during an interview with a local resident Ludwig Citek. He had arrived in Britain as a Ukrainian refugee, and in 1946 was employed within one of the Ordnance Clearing teams. Their task was to clear those parts of the United Kingdom that had been contaminated by military activity. Whilst stationed near Storrington, Citek recalls a particularly difficult task which involved clearing a field at Springhead Hill - a field which, perhaps unsurprisingly, has since been known locally as the Tank Field! He recalls that at the top of the field they found a battered and abandoned Churchill, surrounded by spent rounds, unexploded shells and dud PIAT projectiles. Gradually, as 1946 passed this area was decontaminated. The tank was dealt with by simply using a bulldozer to tip it over into an adjacent shell crater. The tracks were removed and thrown in alongside the tank, now lying upside down on its turret. The last of our Churchills, **11**, is pictured on the Sennybridge Ranges in Wales. It was located on the same disused anti-tank range

wrecker's blades dug in and arrested this movement, the Foden began to rear up on its back wheels. Thankfully, as the front wheels spun in clear air, one of the soldiers realised what was happening! A second attempt with both of the Fodens also ended in drama. As the whine of the winch motors increased in pitch, what sounded like a gunshot rang out. The chain gave way under the pressure and pieces of chain link flew through the air like shrapnel, sending the onlookers diving for cover. After much spadework, the third and final attempt ended in the picture shown here. In **picture 10** we are looking

11

as the Buffalo (page 10). Substantial targets such as these are much in demand. This vehicle was moved to a new anti-tank facility and continued to serve as a target until numerous hits rendered it virtually destroyed (bearing in mind the substantial construction of these vehicles, this is a testament to the power of modern anti-tank weapons). It has recently replaced with a Chieftain.

THE SEXTON

The Sexton, **12**, full designation being '25-pounder, self-propelled, tracked, Sexton', was a Canadian development. Based upon a converted Ram chassis, the first prototype was built in late 1942, with production commencing in early 1943 at the Montreal Locomotive Tank Arsenal. It was, without doubt, the most important tracked Canadian military vehicle to be used in action during the Second World War. By 1944 it had become the mainstay of the self-propelled artillery units in both the Canadian and British armies, and remained so until the end of the war. Specimen **13** is one of a group of Sextons on Salisbury Plain. These vehicles are known to have retained their 25pdr guns up until the seventies, but which have, unfortunately, since been removed. The Sexton, of whom 2,150 were built, remained in British service until 1955. In 1977 India, Italy, Portugal and South Africa were still using it. The Sexton, **14**, is in possession of a little more of its superstructure than the previous examples. On production models this was supplied in the form of welded armour plating with an open top. Should the weather deteriorate, then the 6-man crew was supplied with a canvas cover. Pictured in 2001, this is perhaps the most complete of the Sextons that lie on Salisbury Plain. They all rest in the impact area (the restricted target area). One of the most interesting features is that the base of the gun

12

13

9

mounting, visible at the top of the sloping front glacis plate, is still present. The Sexton was a base for the excellent British 25-pounder field gun, which was mounted slightly left of centre.

THE BUFFALO

spent projectiles, used to lay around. The section of the range were it resided had been disused as an anti-tank range and as part of a tidy-up exercise, the Buffalo, **15 and 16**, as a redundant target, was removed and scrapped. Unfortunately at the time (despite efforts), no interest could be generated to

This example of a Buffalo tracked amphibious carrier, (LVT - Landing Vehicle Tracked), until a few years ago could have been found on the Sennybridge Ranges in Wales. It had been used as a practice anti-tank target and had found the attentions of more than a few 3.5 inch anti tank rockets and 84mm Carl Gustav anti-tank rounds. The evidence for this, in the form of

preserve the vehicle. This vehicle is believed to have been an LVT 3 variant, as it was fitted with twin Cadillac Engines (as opposed to the single Continental radial of other marks) mounted in the sides of the vehicle. The British Army is known to have used LVT 4 & LVT 1 variants, this example was originally painted in a grey colour scheme, perhaps

17

indicating a naval lineage. The LVT 3 variant was produced in 1944 and first used in action on Okinawa. **Picture 17** shows it in the disposal compound awaiting removal as scrap.

THE JAGDPANTHER

A surprise find on the Aldershot ranges, **18**. This German Jagdpanther (Sdkfz173) was believed to have been an un-completed model at the end of the war. It is thought its manufacture was completed by the British and was shipped to this country, presumably for evaluation. When its days had ended as an evaluation vehicle is was being utilised to tow

another tank to an anti-tank range at Aldershot, when it caught fire and was subsequently abandoned. It ended its days as a target on an anti-tank range. This vehicle was removed from the range some years ago and ended up in Germany. It has now returned to this country and undergoing a total restoration. Weighing 51 tons, the Jagdpanther, **21**, was a formidable vehicle, armed with a 8.8cm PaK43 L/71 gun and powered by a 700 HP V12 Maybach HL230P30, V-12 engine. The Jagdpanther was the most successful variation of the Panther tank. Like its parent vehicle the Jagdpanther was a formidable vehicle. On the 30th July 1944, as an example, three Jagdpanthers from the 654 Heavy Anti-Tank Battalion knocked out over a half a squadron of 15 British Churchills in a little over a minute. The design work, instigated in early 1943, followed the standard German practice of using a tank chassis to mount a heavier gun in a limited traverse mounting. This helped keep the overall weight of the vehicle within sensible limits, thereby creating a highly mobile and yet heavily armed 'tank hunter'. The gun was capable of penetrating 22cm of armour, angled at 30 degrees, from a distance of 500 yards. Sixty rounds were carried on board to supply this gun. However, the ammunition was renowned as being heavy and

18

11

difficult to manhandle. As a result the crew of the Jagdpanther, six in total, included two loaders! Alongside the loaders were the commander, a gunner, the wireless operator and a driver. His weapon was a ball-mounted 7.92mm MG34 machine-gun, which would have been fitted in the mounting that can be seen on the left-hand side of the front sloping glacis plate, **19**. The sheer weight of the Jagdpanther required a particularly powerful engine, **Picture 20**. This view was taken looking forward from inside the fighting compartment, and shows the massive construction of the gearbox and final drive units.

Kind permission of Mr. T. Chance

22

THE STURMGESCHUTZ

Hiding behind a Silver Birch is the hulk of a Sturmgeschutz III, or 'Stug' as it is more commonly referred to. The Stug was one of Germany's most enduring armoured vehicles during the Second World War. In this picture, **22**, you are looking at the front of the tank. The tree is actually indicating the rough position where the gun would once have been. Note also the protected drivers viewing slit to the right of the tree trunk. Production of the type started in 1940, and the end of the war produced some 10,500 of the different models. The most common variant was the Ausfuhrung A/G. The Ausf.G. assault guns were widely produced from late 1942. Originally under the control of the artillery arm, they were soon rearranged into battalions consisting of 3 batteries of six vehicles. Assault guns were considered the elite of artillery units, and indeed had a pretty impressive record. By the early months of 1944, these German vehicles, basically self-propelled guns, had claimed some 20,000 enemy tanks destroyed! The Stug was smaller than the Jagdpanther, being based on the PzKpfw III, and weighed in at 23.5 tons, was crewed by four, and had a range of 105 miles. This specimen

used to reside in the same part of the Aldershot ranges as the Jagdpanther. The Stug served not only in the German army, but also with many other Axis countries. Romania, Bulgaria and Hungary used examples on the Eastern Front. Indeed, it is known that some were still in service with Finland and Syria in the late sixties. This vehicle has now been removed and is in private ownership in the UK.

THE COMET

The Comet tanks featured in this book all reside within the restricted impact areas on Salisbury Plain. This type of tank came into service late in the war. They continued in service until the early sixties. This probably accounts for the number that still reside on Salisbury Plain as, though they are of WW2 lineage, they probably became targets relatively recently. The pictures here show different examples in varying conditions. As with all range targets, some seem to fare worse than others. This often governed by the use that the particular area in which the vehicle resides is put, where impact areas fall in and out of use, and also by the type of weapons in service. The Comet tank, (designation A34), came in to service in

23

39mph. Some examples on Salisbury Plain still retain their engines. The design work was undertaken by Leyland Motors, with the first production models available in 1944. The type was basically a complete redesign of the earlier Cromwell tank, and indeed the Comet was to prove to be the last, and best, of the British cruiser tanks, with examples remaining in service worldwide for many years, displaying a remarkable longevity. In 1977 it could still be found at work in countries such as Burma, Eire, Finland and South Africa. The Comet was considered to be an interim vehicle, to be used until the arrival of the heavier Centurion. Despite this, the Comet remained in front-line service in Britain until 1960, and for many years after in reserve. **Picture 23** shows a view from inside a Comet's turret. The view of the rolling downland, normally only seen from such a position through a periscope, is courtesy of a direct hit that has opened up the top of the turret. The barrel of the 17pdr gun can clearly be seen. The designers of the Comet, **24 and 25**, carried over many of the best features of the Cromwell. This included all-welded construction for the hull and turret (found in later Cromwell variants); the Besa machine-gun mounts and the Christie suspension system. Perhaps the most important inheritance, however, was the engine.

December 1944. Its main armament was a "compact" version of the 17pdr anti-tank gun. It had a 5-man crew comprising commander, gunner, loader, driver & co-driver. It was powered by a Rolls-Royce Meteor engine (basically a de-tuned Merlin, less supercharger), with a maximum speed of

24

THE JEEP

Hidden amongst the overgrowth and brambles the pistons, **26**, are almost all that remains of a wartime Jeep. A short walk from the South Downs Way brings you to this location on the South Downs above the village of Storrington in West Sussex. Despite the fact that many local residents still recall tales of its presence, their memory of its exact location has faded in recent years. It was only rediscovered by chance when, on the third and final trip to try and find it, one of the party decided to disappear into a copse to answer a call of nature. Imagine his surprise when, on looking down, he realised that he was standing next to the Jeep remains! Legend has it that the Jeep was badly damaged by troops during exercises leading upto the D-Day landings and was left insitu as a new, softskin, target. What is present indicates that the Jeep now lies upside down. In this picture one can see the front axle, part of the chassis and some pistons that poke out from what there is left of the engine block. A bit of digging also shows that part of the upper body work still remains, though badly decayed and buried beneath the chassis. In July 1940 the United States Army issued a requirement for a new combat truck that was to be capable of carrying a 600lb pay-load, but which also weighed less than 1300lbs itself! This procurement order resulted in perhaps one of the most lasting

images of the Second World War, serving in every Allied army and remaining in service well into the 1950s. By the time the two main manufacturers, Willys MB and Ford, finished production some 639,245 examples had been built. As well as these two American companies, the Jeep was also constructed in 26 foreign plants. The only dispute that still overshadows the Jeep, or Truck 1/4 ton Utility, is the origin of its name. One theory is that the name Jeep had its origins back in the 1930s. At this time several experimental US military multi-purpose vehicles were called 'Jeep' after the Popeye cartoon character. Others feel that Jeep is an acronym of the term General Purpose, or GP, that was applied to the Jeep during its development. What cannot be questioned is the fact that the Jeep made a profound contribution to the Allied war effort.

DEFENSIVE STRUCTURES

It was not only redundant hardware that was used as range targets. In many locations mock-up defensive structures were built for the specific purpose of military training. One structure that suffered this most ignominious fate was a pillbox built on the South Downs above Worthing in West Sussex by Canadian Army Engineers. Now an extremely overgrown mass of crumbled concrete and bent reinforcing rods, so damaged that its original shape is lost, this pillbox suffered the fate of being shelled by its own side! In the build up to the Overlord landings the Canadian Forces used it as a range target. It was subjected to fire by 2" and 3" mortar - evidenced by the fact that the field around it is a carpet of fuse caps, shrapnel and twisted mortar fins. The structure in **picture 27** is an example that can be seen on Salisbury Plain. Note how the concrete has gradually been blasted away from the steel reinforcing rods, leaving them standing rusted and mangled.

27

16

28

THE M3 LEE/GRANT

Another Aldershot target, **28**, on an anti-tank range, shows evidence of plenty of use! By 1940, with the German blitzkrieg in full swing, the United States had a moment of panic. At this time it possessed the meagre total of just 18 modern medium tanks! New designs were rapidly sought, with the Medium M3 being the result. For the first time the enormous resources of the American automotive industries were unleashed and an initial order for 1,000 was placed. By the time that production was switched to the M4 Sherman, some 5,000 Lee/Grants had been completed. In the meantime the British purchasing mission to the United States had ordered this tank in huge quantities, and it is almost certain that the tank pictured here is from that order. This picture clearly shows the double turret design of the M3. The main armament, a 75mm gun, was placed in the hull-mounted turret - on the left of this hull. This turret displayed one of the major faults of the M3 in that this main gun could only be traversed through 30 degrees. The top turret, did have a full 360 degree field of fire, but was only equipped with the 37mm gun. Various machine guns were also fitted in the hull

and turrets, though the exact calibre and number depended on the variant. To cope with such an array of weapons, the M3 required a crew of six. The M3, known as the Grant by the British, first saw use by their forces in 1942 serving throughout the Middle and Far East.

SOFT SKIN VEHICLES

Soft skinned vehicles rarely fare well on ranges. As most of these ranges are in areas of exposed upland, these more fragile targets are subject to the ravages of extreme weather as well as the direct action of military ordnance. On the Sennybridge ranges in Wales in 1955, it was decided that the Artillery practice area (as it was then) was somewhat devoid of decent targets. To rectify that a number of redundant WW2 vintage lorries were obtained as targets and placed on the range during January 1955. These vehicles varied in type (Austin, Bedford, Fordson). The remains of these vehicles still reside on the range today. The vehicle in **picture 29** is a post war AEC Militant. A rare example of another soft skinned vehicle, the Bedford MW, still resides on the Sennybridge ranges, **30**. It is believed that this is an

17

MW type, as opposed to the bigger OY series (which had the same radiator grill), by comparison of the chassis sizes. Little is known of the history of these vehicles. All the lorry targets on Sennybridge have well worn and varied tyres fitted (some with sand tyres). On some of the tyres fitted to these vehicles the letters 'WD', a broad arrow mark and dates of 1944/45 can still be made out. The prototype of the Bedford MW made its first appearance in 1937, and was based on a commercial 2-ton truck. More than 65,000 of these 4 x 2 15-cwt trucks were produced from 1939 to 1945. It was powered by a Bedford 6-cylinder petrol Engine.

THE TEA-HOUSE

One of the vehicles that arrived in 1955 was a Bedford QL. This particular vehicle was an ex-NAAFI

tea wagon. It was utilised as an Observation Post vehicle and given the nickname "The teahouse of the august moon", after the 1956 film starring Marlon Brando. There are, no doubt, many ex-national serviceman 'Gunners' who remember this vehicle, **31**. This vehicle can still be seen today residing on a hill above one of the field firing areas, **32**.

The Bedford QL (4x4 3 ton) went into production in 1940. More than 50,000 were produced between 1940 & 1945. Powered by a 3.5 litre straight 6-cylinder petrol engine, it had a range of 230 miles. The Bedford QL (4x4, 3 ton) went into production in 1940, and was to be the first major mainstream 4x4 truck developed by a British company. Indeed, American manufactured lorries supplied under Lend-Lease inspired the development of such a vehicle.

More than 52,000 were produced between 1940 and 1945, almost all by Vauxhall Motors at their Luton plant. Such a high figure was achieved despite the fact that making a 4x4 required a third more manpower again as a comparable 4x2. With a range of 230 miles, the QL became the most common British 3-ton military truck of the Second World War. Picture **33** shows another unidentified type, though clearly fitted with a tipper body on the back. Note the bullet holes in the front tyre that is sticking up into the air (circled).

THE CRUSADER

Located amongst the long grass on Salisbury Plain is a rather rare tank, **34**, particularly in terms of range targets. Despite looking sadly all the worse for wear this is an example of a Crusader, the most important British operational cruiser tank of the 1941-1942 period. Designed by the Nuffield organisation, full blown production had got underway by the dark days of 1940. Built from a combination of riveted and bolted steel, the Crusader was armed with a 2-pounder gun and a 7.92mm machine-gun. On board

the 5 man crew (on the Mk I) had a supply of 110 rounds for the 2-pounder, and 4,500 for the machine-gun. In total, 5,300 examples of the type were built. As the Crusader also proved a suitable base for a number of specialised roles, 1,373 advanced beyond the standard cruiser tank. There were turret-less bulldozer and recovery versions; some became artillery observation posts, whilst others were developed into armoured tractors for 17-pounder artillery pieces. Despite a number of faults the Crusader was generally a successful design, proving particularly valuable in the North African campaign. Indeed, there are many who feel that had the Crusader been strategically and tactically better employed then it could have made a much more useful contribution to the British military effort.

THE DAIMLER ARMOURED CARS

Daimler armoured cars are known to exist on a number of ranges. These armoured cars were purpose built, as opposed to previous armoured cars, which had been derived from other vehicles (and would be again with the Humber Pig). Powered by a straight six 95bhp Daimler engine, the Daimler was armed with a 2-pdr gun for main armament, **35**, and

a 7.92mm BESA machine gun as secondary armament. The vehicles pictured here are all on the Sennybridge ranges. A number of these vehicles existed here, but many have now gone, removed for restoration, complete or cannibalised for spare parts. When a range development necessitated the removal of some, one was found to have its engine still wrapped in preservative covering, having covered no miles since its last re-build. A number of these vehicles also used to exist on Salisbury Plain until the mid-nineties. However, it is not known what happened to these. Many range vehicles provide valuable spare parts for museum and privately owned restorations. In **picture 36** a wheel station is being removed from this Daimler hulk. One such restoration of a Daimler armoured car has been carried out with outstanding results. One can only marvel at the amount of dedication and work involved in restoring an armoured fighting vehicle. The restoration featured here is of a Mk 2 Daimler. This vehicle was recovered from the Lydd ranges in approximately 1982 as scrap. It was then transferred to a West Country museum and featured as part of a diorama. The present owner saw it in the yard at the back of the museum in 1991 and persuaded the

35

owner to part with it for restoration. After much hard work and a lot of money it was finally taxed in 1997. From what can be seen of these vehicles, it appears that most are Mark II versions. At its inception, Daimler designed these armoured cars to the theory of 'Tank, Light and wheeled'. The desire was to produce a vehicle that combined performance, armament and armour in an easily and cheaply manufactured package - at the same time attempting to equal some of the light tanks of the period. After some initial hurdles, the Daimler products turned into some of the best and most capable armoured cars of the Second World War. The Mark II was an evolution of the initial Mark I, and at a quick glance both look quite similar. Those changes that were made came about as a result of experience in the field. Visual differences include the addition of a driver's escape hatch in the hull roof; a new radiator and grill; and a new gun mantlet. Both sourced the same 95hp rear mounted six-cylinder engine, (generating a top road speed of 50mph), though the Mark II did see the introduction of a 2-speed dynamo. The next two photographs, **37 and 38**, graphically illustrate the sheer work involved in such projects. The second, **38**, was taken just before the armoured car was moved for the start of the restoration. We are looking down

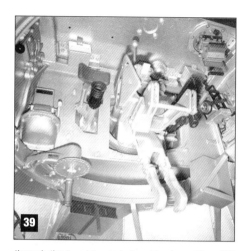

through the turret towards the driver's position. Still recognisable, though only just, are the driver's seat, steering wheel and a number of the instruments along the front of the hull. Having received restoration the hull and turret emerge as if new (if not better) - **pictures 39 and 40**. No detail is spared right down to the gun sight, leather padding and even the first aid kit mounted just in front of the turret ring! The completely restored Daimler, **41**, immaculately turned out - fully taxed and tested! Such work is a credit to its owner and a fitting tribute to all those who served in these vehicles. Thanks to projects like this, living history continues as one of the 2,694 Mark I and IIs built, remains for future generations.

All pictures kind permission of Mr. Bob Stephens

42

AIRCRAFT

It is not only redundant vehicles that end up on military ranges, many aircraft do as well. The Gloster Meteor pictured here is one of two that reside at Sennybridge. The Meteor entered service with the RAF in July 1944 with 616 squadron and was to be the only operational jet fighter that served in an Allied air force throughout the Second World War. The Meteor had initially been pressed into service in an attempt to counter the V1 flying bomb threat. This aircraft, **42**, with the serial number VZ 568, is an F.8

single seat day fighter variant built by Armstrong Whitworth Aviation. This variant of Meteor first flew with the RAF in 1949 and was the mainstay of RAF fighter command between 1950 and 1955. This version is powered by Rolls Royce Derwent turbo jet engines and could reach a speed of 600 Mph. It was this variant that served with the R.A.A.F. in Korea. The F.8 variant was a popular test-bed aircraft. This may explain why this aircraft evaded the scrapman as it may have had a long career serving in a test establishment. In the second photograph, **43**, more

43

44

detail of the aircraft can be seen. On the left is the barren engine nacelle that would once have housed one of the aircraft's pair of Rolls-Royce Derwent turbo-jet engines. Equipment included the Martin-Baker ejector seat, part of the fittings for which are visible at the rear of the cockpit. Note also the housing at the front of the nose, where two of the four Hispano 20mm cannon were fitted to the Meteor. One interesting feature still present inside the cockpit, is the use of wood fittings. More for the aviation enthusiast can be seen in **picture 44**! This English Electric Canberra, looking like an aircraft that has just crashed, was one of the type designed by W.E.W 'Teddy' Petter. The Canberra first took to the air on the 13th May 1949 and soon gained a reputation for its deftness in spite of its 6,000lb (2722kg) bomb-load. By the time it had entered into Bomber Command service in 1951 the Canberra excelled in intercepting fighters due to its sheer agility. This two-seat light bomber and intruder was capable of a top speed of 580 mph and, in its basic form, was equipped with four 20mm Hispano cannon and four 1,000lb bombs. The English Electric Canberra engendered 20 basic variants for use in British service and still more for export, serving in countries such as Venezuela, New Zealand, Peru and India. Note the RAF roundel on the wing that lies to the left of the main nose section.

THE SHERMAN

Sherman tanks are common as targets on military ranges. Many can still be found today in various conditions and locations. To describe the development and history of the Sherman would be impossible here. It did, however, come around as the result of the need to replace the M3 Lee/Grant, which had always been intended as an interim vehicle. Like most of the M4s pictured, the one in **picture 45** can be found on the rolling downland of Salisbury Plain. For the enthusiast, it is actually an M4A2 variant. These models were supplied with a welded hull, and powered by the General Motors 6046 diesel engine (which was, basically, two civilian truck engines bolted together!). The example in **picture 46** is in

45

remarkably good condition, even to the extent that it has retained one of its tracks. As the M4 developed, it became fitted with a wide range of armament. In the original form, the M4 was equipped with a 75mm M3 gun with a coaxial 0.30" Browning machine-gun. In the front of the hull was another Browning in a ball mounting and, beside this, two further fixed forward firing guns. The short appearance of the gun on this Sherman is not due to it having been cut down, but the fact that it has slipped back on its mounting into the turret. Little is known about the origins and fate of the Sherman in **picture 47**, other than the fact that it was photographed in the late 1980's resting in a quiet corner of a Kent scrapyard. Examination of the hull suggests that it served, at some stage, as a

range target. The telltale bullet strikes are scattered across the front of the hull and sides of the turret. Visible in this picture, on the bottom left of the hull front, is the ball mounting that would have carried the .30 Browning machine gun. **Pictures 48 and 49** show two vehicles in particularly good condition. One of these, on Salisbury Plain, can be found hiding amongst the undergrowth. Unsurprisingly, the Sherman is possibly one, if not the most common of the tank sourced range targets. No doubt this is the result of the sheer number of these tanks that were built. By the time production ground to a halt in 1945, the colossal figure of over 58,000 units had been

49

manufactured. The Sherman served worldwide and even in 1987 could still be found hard at work. Israel kept the type in service as the Super Sherman and Isherman, though up-rated with new engines and armaments. Examples could also be seen in many Latin-American nations, in Portugal, Uganda and, at that time, Yugoslavia.

THE FUNNIES

Along with the German vehicles some of the rarest surviving range targets are the two 'Funnies' illustrated here. "Funnies" was the collective term given to the specialist armoured-vehicles used on D-day (and beyond) designed and built under the stewardship of Major General Percy Hobart. Hobart was appointed as Montgomery's Specialized Armour (Hobart was Montgomery's brother in-law). The "funnies", so named by the Americans and largely

rejected by them, played a major part in the campaigns in NW Europe during WW2. The first, **50**, is a Churchill Crocodile, whilst the second, **52**, is a Churchill bridge-layer. The Churchill Crocodile was a tank-mounted flame-thrower used by the British Army during the Second World War. It was a weapon that was most effective, and was found to be extremely demoralising to those enemy soldiers that had to face their onslaught. The standard Churchill Crocodile consisted of a Mark VII Churchill tank that had the flame nozzle replacing the hull mounted Besa machine gun. The fuel for the flame-thrower was stored in an armoured trailer that was towed behind the tank. The trailer was joined to the tank by a newly developed link that was hinged to allow as much movement as possible. Like the trailer this link, which can be seen sticking up at the back of this range target, was also armoured. From this link the

50

51

52

fuel was carried through a pipe under the tank, before passing out of the internal nozzle mounting. The latter can be seen in picture **51**. In the centre of the picture the pipe can be seen coming up from the floor and joining the actual firing nozzle. The fuel was ejected from this nozzle, which could be directed like the hull machine-gun it replaced, in short bursts or in a prolonged and continuous jet of flame (which would have lasted a maximum of around 80 seconds). Another adaptation of the basic Churchill tank is shown in **52**, and is more properly known as the A.V.R.E. (Assault Vehicle, Royal Engineers) SBG Bridge Carrier. The SBG was the Small Box Girder

bridge which was designed to carry a 40ton load when deployed. The introduction of this design meant that a 30 foot road bridge could be deployed quickly under enemy fire. On the front of the tank, pictured, can still be seen part of the mechanical arm that was used to deploy the bridge.

PANTHER TURRET

This one time range target, **53**, and which is now on display in the Tank Museum at Bovington, is indeed something of a rarity. For nearly fifty years it lay as a hard target on the artillery range at Larkhill. Then, almost by chance, it was realised that this 'lump of

53

Kind permission of The Tank Museum

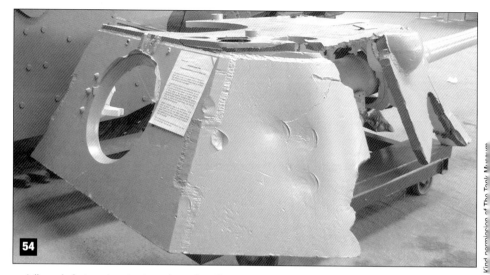

54

metal' was in fact an almost unique piece of wartime history. In 1944 the German High Command issued instructions that were intended to further develop the legendary Panther tank series. This new model, the Panther Ausf. F., was to inherit the same hull, but be given a totally new design of turret. This new turret was to have a much-reduced front facing, providing a narrower target in the event of a frontal attack. This reduction also meant that the engineers could introduce a valuable increase in turret armour thickness without adding to the overall weight of the whole tank. Daimler-Benz began production at its factories, but was almost immediately brought to a halt by allied air attacks. Indeed, no examples of this type were ever completed in time to see active service. When the Allied armies finally overran the Daimler-Benz works just two completed examples of the new turret design were found. One went to the United States, and this is the other! Evidence of the hard life that this turret underwent is only too visible. The prolonged exposure to artillery fire has created the typical results of 'Behind Armour Effects' inside the turret, **54**. Closer inspection also reveals some of the new features that the turret was to incorporate. On each of the corners of the turret can be seen mortise joints. By joining the main armour plates in this way the German designers increased the turret strength by lengthening the weld. On each side of the turret is a bulge - somewhat like a frog's eye! These were

intended to house a stereoscopic range finder, newly designed by the German optical manufacturer Zeiss. The gun, shortened on the Bovington example for convenience, was basically the same 75mm used on the earlier Panthers but updated with a new recoil system.

THE VALENTINE

As the Valentine tank soon became outmoded during the war, it ceased to be used as a first line tank and was utilised for training. Some obviously found their way to ranges as targets. Complete tanks and the remains of tanks can be found on Sennybridge, Aldershot and disused ranges in Surrey & Sussex. No doubt others exist elsewhere - indeed at the time of writing, 2001, the author lives on the south coast and one resides under the water not far off the beach where he lives. The hulks pictured here all reside on the Sennybridge ranges. In total 10 Valentines exist at Sennybridge. It is rumoured that these tanks were placed here during the war as targets for rocket firing Typhoons. This may well be the case as these hulks are all badly damaged. Due to the nature of construction of these tanks however, (riveted rather than welded construction), when directly hit, they tend to spring apart. The result of this is that often a tank hulk may look completely destroyed, but in fact is still lying around but in "kit" form. When one of these hulks was being

cannibalised to provide parts for a restoration, when scraping the earth (and sheep residue) from the fighting compartment, the gun cleaning kit came to light, consisting of tools and wire brushes. Whether this had been overlooked or was sent to the range with some of its equipment still intact we probably will never know. The tank in **picture 56** still retains its serial number (T61008) painted on the right hand driver's hatch. In picture **55**, a frontal view of a Valentine, minus its turret, one can see the driver's viewing slit on the vertical section of the hull front. Much discussion has been made around the origin of the Valentine's name. The most favoured answer centres on the fact that the original plans for the

type were placed before the War Office by Vickers a couple of days prior to Valentines Day, 1938. The Valentine's method of construction did provide the stretched British wartime manufacturers with one advantage - time. It took one-third less man-hours to build a Valentine than the Matilda. Indeed more Valentine tank chassis were constructed than any other British model throughout the entire war. Near this tank the substantial remains of a 7.2" Howitzer shell were found. To the un-initiated this is a VERY large shell and probably accounts for the severe damage to the vehicles in the vicinity. In **picture 57**, we are looking at the rear of a Valentine showing an empty engine bay.

THE POST WAR DESIGNS

On almost every current military range you will find a selection of many post-war British military designs - including complete tanks, but is more likely to be armoured personnel carriers or armoured cars. The pictures that follow provide the reader with a selection of these vehicles. The first, **58**, is of a design that, until recently, would have been familiar to those who frequently watched the national news. This is the Humber 1 Ton Armoured Truck or FV1611. However, to those who have served in these vehicles they are more affectionately known as the Humber 'Pig'. This 4x4 armoured vehicle was developed by Humber who used the chassis of one of their civilian models as the base. Powered by a Rolls-Royce 6-cylinder petrol engine, these 'Pigs', so called because of their size and appalling handling characteristics, could only manage about 45mph on the open road. Weighing 5790kg, they had a crew of two and could carry up to 8 additional troops. The 'Pigs' were widely used by the British Army, and served with distinction

59

in Northern Ireland until being replaced by the Saxon armoured car. The vehicle shown here is an ex-Northern Ireland vehicle, sporting the large grill bars added at the front as an anti-barricade/riot-protection measure. This vehicle is one of a batch delivered from the army's Central Vehicle Depot, which used to be located at Ludgershall, as targets.

Wales, this is a particularly battered target, and can be seen minus its front axle - as well as much bodywork! The development of the FV603 Alvis Saracen began shortly after the end of World War Two, with the first examples being completed in 1952. Sharing many components with the Stalwart, production continued for an impressive twenty years. Built at the time when British armament companies were globally dominant, the Saracen was an export success. In time it would be sold to over 16 countries, including nations like Brunei, Nigeria, Thailand, Qatar and Indonesia. Hong Kong placed orders for specially designed examples for Police work, whilst those sold to Kuwait were open topped versions. Returning to tracked AVs we come to the FV432 armoured personnel carrier, **61**. Built by J. Sankey, the 432 is a lightweight fully tracked vehicle providing armoured protection to infantry detachments. The hull is constructed of steel armoured plate of sufficient thickness to give protection against shell fragments, flash burns and small arms fire. The integrity and strength of the armoured body can actually be seen in **picture 61**, on Sennybridge range. On the side and front are a number of patches, indicating strike marks.

Our next type, **59**, is the immediately identifiable Stalwart. More of a mouthful is the correct military designation for this vehicle - Truck Cargo HMLC, FV622 Alvis Stalwart 6x6! Manufactured by Alvis Co. Ltd. in Coventry it is basically an amphibious and cross-country high mobility load carrier whose design and manufacture began in the early sixties. Like the Humber 'Pigs', this Stalwart can be found on the Sennybridge ranges.

Next on the list of post-war types is an Alvis Saracen armoured personnel carrier, or APC - **60**. Located in

To finish with is a picture, **62**, of a range target that is something of a mystery! It is thought that the superstructure is a mock-up fitted to the hull which resides on Salisbury Plain. What is known is that the base vehicle that has been used was a Centurion. The Centurion Main Battle Tank was developed during the final years of the Second World War, though the first prototype was not completed until late 1945. It is likely that this was used as a trials vehicle, but for what is unknown.

Answers on a post card please!

62

www.historicmilitarypress.com